MW01610017

Lifelong Learning

Why it's more important and doable than you think

Don McMinn

iPlace Press

TABLE OF CONTENTS

Chapter 1 > **5**

Lifelong learning is more important than you think

Chapter 2 > **15**

Eleven prerequisites for lifelong learning

Chapter 3 > **31**

Lifelong learning is more doable than you think —
10 actions that will enhance your learning

Chapter 4 > **51**

How to get maximum benefit from reading

1 LIFELONG LEARNING IS MORE IMPORTANT THAN YOU THINK

In Gail Godwin's novel, *The Finishing School*, 44-year-old Ursula teaches 14-year-old Justin the difference between people who grow stale in life and those who remain vital.

> "There are two kinds of people . . . One kind, you can tell just by looking at them at what point they congealed into their final selves. It might be a very *nice* self, but you know you can expect no more surprises from it. Whereas, the other kind keeps moving, changing. That doesn't mean they're unstable. Ah, no, far from it. They are *fluid*. They keep moving forward and making new trysts with life, and the motion of it keeps them young. In my opinion, they are the only people who are still alive."

There was a time in my life when I temporarily "congealed into my final self."

I finished my Ph.D. degree when I was 27 years old, so the first decade of my adult life was intellectually robust. But then I punched pause on my pursuit of learning, and for the next 10 years I was intellectually disengaged and became increasingly stale.

Perhaps I suffered from "destination disease," which John Maxwell describes as, "Some people mistakenly believe that if they can accomplish a particular goal, they no longer have to grow. This disease can infect us at many times in life: after earning a degree, reaching a desired position, receiving a particular award, or achieving a financial goal."[1]

Fortunately, I discovered the antidote for destination disease—lifelong learning. Bennis & Goldsmith teach, "The act of committing oneself to being a lifelong learner can take place at any point in one's life."[2] I'm very glad I made the commitment.

Here are five good reasons to be a lifelong learner.

1. Lifelong learning will help you cultivate vision.

There is a scene in Lewis Carroll's *Alice in Wonderland* where Alice is talking to the Cheshire Cat, who is perched up in a tree. Alice is a bit confused about her direction, so she asks the cat:

> "Would you tell me, please, which way I ought to go from here?"

> "That depends a great deal on where you want to go," replies the Cheshire cat.

> "I don't much care where," says Alice.

> To which the feline replies, "Then it doesn't matter which way you go."

Some people face the same predicament as Alice. They don't really know which way they want to go in life, so they just wander aimlessly and soon become stagnant and stale.

But that's no way to live. "Que sera, sera. Whatever will be, will be" may be a cute song to sing but it's a lousy philosophy on which to build your life. The old adage, "If you aim at nothing, you will always hit it," is sad but true.

The solution to this problem is fresh vision.

Vision is a picture of the future that is better than the present. It is a clear and credible depiction of a better tomorrow. Vision gives us direction and motivates us to pursue a better reality.

But where does vision come from? What is the optimum environment in which vision is spawned?

Vision favors an engaged, well-informed mind. It is often found "along the way" of a curious, ever-expanding journey. As we engage in fresh encounters, we see things we normally would not see, and we begin to visualize new opportunities.

For me, vision often forms as a compilation of various and unrelated parts. I'll notice something in a museum, read a thought in a magazine, and hear something in a conversation; then there is a moment when the formerly unrelated parts coalesce into a new entity. It is a splendid experience, made possible by living a life that is constantly exposed to multiple, intellectual stimuli.

2. Lifelong learning will keep you current.

The rate of change in society has dramatically increased. Clarke and Crossland comment on this rapid rate of change in their book *The Leader's Voice*: "In ancient times, work was performed on an almost stationary stage. Visionary inventor Ray Kurzweil explains the rate of change in terms of paradigm shifts. During the agricultural age, paradigm shifts occurred over thousands of years. The industrial age produced paradigm shifts, first in a century and then in a generation. At the start of the information age, paradigms appeared to shift at the rate of three per lifetime. Kurzweil suggests that beginning in the year 2000, paradigm shifts have begun to occur at the rate of seven to ten per lifetime."[3]

This rapid rate of change makes lifelong learning essential, because if you're not growing and learning, you will quickly become antiquated and obsolete.

I hesitate to cite the following data because it became outdated even as I typed it. But focus on the implication of each statement, realizing that the specific facts are constantly changing.

The quantity of knowledge is expanding exponentially.

- 3,000 books are published daily.

- 80% of all the scientists and engineers who have ever lived are alive today.

- The CEO at Google says we are now creating as much data every two days as we did from the dawn of time to 2003.

- More knowledge exists in one weekend edition of The New York Times than the average person had access to in their entire lifetime in the 1800s.

- 1.5 exabytes of information will be created this year. (The prefix exa means one billion billion.) That's more than was created in the previous 5,000 years.

The U.S. is being challenged in its role as a world leader.

- Both China and India have more honor students than the U.S. has students.

- The U.S. ranks 20th in the world for broadband penetration.

- China will soon have more English speakers in their population than any other country in the world.

- The U.S. now ranks 25th in math, 17th in science, and 14th in reading out of the 34 countries that comprise the Organization for Economic Cooperation and Development (OECD).

It is more difficult to excel in life than ever before.

In his must-read book, *Talent is Overrated*, Geoff Colvin gives two examples that illustrate how difficult it has become to excel in life.

> "The winner of the men's 200-meter race in the 1908 Olympics ran it in 22.6 seconds; today's high school record is faster by more than 2 seconds. Today's top high school athletes run a marathon twenty minutes faster than the Olympic gold medalist did in 1908.

> "When Tchaikovsky finished writing his Violin Concerto in 1878, he asked the famous violinist Leopold Auer to give the premier performance. Auer studied the score and said no—he thought the work was unplayable. Today, most young violinists graduating from a major school of music can play the piece."[4]

In every area of life, the bar is being raised. Yesterday's best is today's norm. Today's norm will soon be subpar. Individuals and organizations will find competing increasingly difficult and surviving impossible if they are not constantly staying fresh. Ongoing success will come from ongoing learning.

3. Lifelong leaning will make you more employable.

Abraham Lincoln said, "If I had six hours to chop down a tree, I would spend two hours sharpening my axe."

His statement reminds us how important it is to keep sharp the tools with which we do our work. Lincoln lived in an agricultural and industrial age, so his statement immediately appealed to the physicality of most people's work.

In the 21st century, most of us are knowledge workers—our "axe" is our mind. The "shelf life" of most technical knowledge is 12 to 18 months; after that it is too dated to be considered cutting edge. To be effective in the workforce, we must keep our minds sharp.

The U.S. Department of Labor estimates that young people entering the workforce today will have 10 to 14 different jobs by their 38th birthday. In the past, a person could meander through his career with no concern for lifelong learning and suffer few consequences, land a job with a major corporation or in a stable industry, and coast for the rest of his life. But in today's fast-changing environment, that simply won't work.

4. Lifelong learning will keep you fresh and appealing.

When I meet someone for the first time, it only takes me about 20 minutes of conversation to determine whether his or her life is stale or fresh.

The symptoms of an atrophied life are obvious: threadbare curiosity, tired vision, unimaginative vocabulary, dated and overused stories, and a slow, almost languid pace.

People who have pushed the pause button on their personal development may someday be described by the fictitious gravestone that reads: "Died, age 45; buried age 70." Quite frankly, those people are uninteresting and lifeless.

But people who are fully alive, current, and vitally engaged with life are interesting to be with and have something to contribute to life and relationships. They provide stimulating conversations and insightful observations. Lifelong learning sustains interesting and growing relationships.

5. Lifelong learning is enjoyable.

The main reason we should be lifelong learners is for the sheer joy of it.

The world is a fascinating place that provides innumerable areas to investigate and explore. Our minds are quickened, engaged, and rewarded when we consider the wonders of God's creation and the exploits of man. Consider the areas of study offered by a major university: anthropology, chemistry, psychology, music, journalism, biology, history, art, architecture, and others. Don't these subjects arouse your curiosity and whet your appetite for learning?

The World Wide Web gives us instant, current access to most of the world's knowledge. Using your computer you can visit any place and investigate any thought, and doing so will ignite your imagination and feed your mind.

I'm 63 years old (as of 2015). I now have more past than I do future. I regret that for several decades I punched the pause button on my learning; I was simply unaware of the pure joy that comes from growing and learning. I can't recover the lost opportunities, but I am committed to live fully till I die, and the core of that pursuit will be to feed an insatiable appetite for learning and growing.

The power of incremental growth

When Albert Einstein was asked what he thought was the human race's greatest invention, he replied, "Compound interest."

There is a big difference between simple and compound interest. Simple interest lets you earn money only on your principal. Compound interest lets you earn money on your principal and your interest. For instance, at a simple interest rate of 10%, it will take 10 years to double your money. A compound interest rate of 10% will double your money in just 7.2 years.

The same advantage that compound interest has on money will also apply to your investment in lifelong learning. The cumulative effect of learning is astonishing.

John Kotter, in his book *Leading Change*, puts it this way:

"Between age thirty and fifty, Fran 'grows' at the rate of 6 percent—that is, every year she expands her career-relevant skills and knowledge by 6 percent. Her twin sister, Janice, has exactly the same intelligence, skills, and information at age thirty, but during the next twenty years she grows at only 1 percent per year. Perhaps Janice becomes smug and complacent after early successes. Or maybe Fran has some experience that sets a fire underneath her. The question here is, how much difference will this relatively small learning differential make by age fifty?

"Given the facts about Fran and Janice, it's clear that the former will be able to do more at age fifty than the latter. But most of us underestimate how much more capable Fran will become. The confusion surrounds the effect of compounding. Just as we often don't realize the difference over 20 years between a bank account earning 7 percent versus 4 percent, we regularly underestimate the effects of learning differentials.

"For Fran and Janice, the difference between a six percent and a one percent growth rate over twenty years is huge. If they each have 100 units of career-related capability at age 30, 20 years later, Janice will have 122 units, while Fran will have 321. Peers at age 30, the two will be in totally different leagues at age 50.

"If the world of the twenty-first century were going to be stable, regulated, and prosperous, sort of like the 1950s and 1960s in the United States, then differential growth rates would be of only modest relevance. In that world, while Fran would likely be considered more accomplished than her sister, both would do just fine. Stability, regulation, and prosperity would reduce competition along with the need for growth in leadership skills, and transformation. But that's not what the future holds."[5]

Steady growth at even a slow rate has enormous long-term impact.

Lifelong learning inventory

Take a few minutes to respond to the following diagnostic assessment. Be frank and honest. You must be truthful for it to be reliable.

1. List the books you have read in the past six months.

2. What is the farthest you have traveled from home in your life? In the past 24 months?

3. Who are your mentors, both distant mentors (people you respect but do not know personally) and personal mentors (people you interact with on a consistent and intentional basis)?

4. Describe the last time you failed.

5. What areas of life are you currently curious about?

6. What words have you recently added to your vocabulary?

7. What have you learned recently that has altered the way you think and/or behave?

8. What have you memorized lately?

Retain your answers; we'll address each of these issues in the following chapters.

2

ELEVEN PREREQUISITES FOR LIFELONG LEARNING

When I became serious about ongoing learning, I discovered some attitudes and actions that will assist and strengthen our pursuit. Here are eleven suggestions that will enhance your ability to learn.

1. Adopt a holistic approach to learning.

We are multi-dimensional beings, so adopt a multi-dimensional approach to lifelong learning. Determine to grow and develop intellectually, emotionally, relationally, professionally, spiritually, and physically.

All six areas are important, and they are interrelated; neglecting one will impinge upon the others, and strengthening one will enhance the others. In other words, your emotional well-being will affect your spiritual well-being which will impact your relationships. Your physical well-being impacts all areas. For instance, I exercise three times a week, once to exhaustion. I don't enjoy doing it, but I'm always glad I did it. I exercise to keep my body in shape so it will enhance, and not hinder, the activity of my mind. I buffet my body so it will serve the higher, more important realms of consciousness.

I strive to be emotionally healthy and intelligent so I can properly respond to human interactions. I want to be spiritually fit so I will understand the transcendent and how it relates to all things.

> > >

Live deep and suck the marrow out.
—Thoreau

> > >

2. Develop an inquiring mind; be curious.

Albert Einstein once said, "I have no special talent. I am only passionately curious." I think he was being excessively modest in the first phrase, but notice his emphasis on curiosity in the second. An inquiring, curious mind is supple, eager, and insatiable.

Will Durant spoke of this intellectual curiosity: "Sixty years ago I knew everything; now I know nothing; education is a progressive discovery of our own ignorance." Curiosity will give us an insatiable appetite for learning and growing.

Ralph Waldo Emerson was reported to have greeted his friends with the question, "What has become more clear to you since we last met?" Emerson was inviting others to share an update on what they were thinking about, and his question was also a subtle test: What if the person didn't have a legitimate answer to that question? What if nothing had become more clear? His question assumes an inquiring and curious mind, one that is constantly developing multiple ideas and thoughts. I think Emerson also anticipated and expected reciprocity in the conversation—he would have the opportunity to share what he was thinking about.

If someone unexpectedly approached you and asked, *"What has become more clear to you since we last met?"* would you have a ready answer that you're eager to discuss?

We should always be coddling and nurturing various thoughts and ideas. Our minds should be an incubator for developing thoughts.

I call this a "thought pipeline," a process in which select thoughts and ideas are constantly being considered and gradually become more mature.

Thought Pipeline

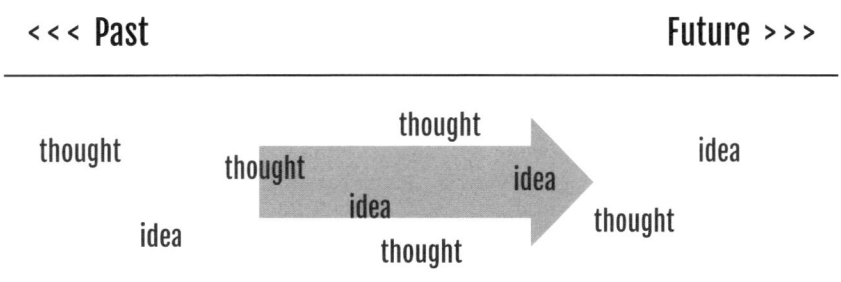

For instance, years ago I was counseling a married couple when it became clear that the relationship was suffering because one spouse was very controlling. I didn't know very much about that topic so I immediately placed it in my thought pipeline. After the session was over I called a respected psychologist friend of mine and asked him to give me a quick lesson on controlling behavior. I invested several hours that week into learning more about the behavior and when I met the couple again, I was able to offer sound advice. That issue—controlling behavior—*is still in my thought pipeline* and continues to mature.

Throughout life we should be entertaining thousands of thoughts that are gradually but continually becoming more clear. It is curiosity that first identifies the topic and places it in the pipeline. Through curiosity we discover new things to love and pursue.

> > >
Asking a question assigns you the task of finding an answer.
—Twyla Tharp

> > >

3. Be willing to pay the price for growing.

There are several "costs" involved in being a lifelong learner. One relates to the environment we are in.

There is a species of fish—the Japanese carp, known as the Koi—that will grow in size only in proportion to the size of the body of water it is in. When placed in a small aquarium, the fish will only grow to be two or three inches long. If placed in a larger body of water, it will grow to six to ten inches. When placed in a large lake, it can reach its full size of two or three feet in length.

In like manner, your environment can inhibit and limit your personal growth and development. It may be the job you're in—although you may feel secure and the work is tolerable, you're stuck in a mind-numbing environment and your head is hitting the proverbial glass ceiling. It may be where you live—the provincial mentality is stifling. The friends you associate with may be stymying—you may need a more intellectually invigorating group.

But the *right* environment can stimulate your growth and help you reach your potential. Fortunately, you *do* have control over these dimensions of life: you can choose where you work, you can move to a city that inspires you, and you can choose friends that will stretch you.

After graduating from college, my daughter Lauren made some bold moves that placed her in a "large pond." First, she moved from a small college town in Texas to New York City. She got a nice and adequate job, but after working there for a few years, she realized she needed a greater challenge so she made the shift to American Express. Soon, AMEX moved her to Singapore for a year, then back to NYC. In the meantime, she completed a master's degree from Columbia. Can you sense the mix of challenges, thrills, fear, insecurity, and joy involved in making these moves? And yet, she did it, and it helped her grow into a large carp. (Sorry, Lauren, I couldn't resist.)

Don't underestimate the courage it takes to change environments and the effort it takes to adjust to and flourish in a new one. It can be intimidating and challenging. You may even fail. But it's worth the risk and effort. Life is too short to waste; it is not a dress rehearsal, and it's the only one you get.

Another cost associated with lifelong learning is the time, energy, and financial resources required.

- What do you do with your discretionary time? Watch TV or read a book? Go shopping for items you don't really need or take a course at your local community college? How you use your free time is very important and a huge predictor of success.

- What do you do with your discretionary money? Will you spend your money on the latest/greatest gadgets or for an international trip?

Your choices and priorities in life will ultimately influence and shape who you are.

4. Take responsibility for your personal growth.

Bennis and Goldsmith say, "Adults learn best when they take charge of their own learning." Actually, I think *everyone* learns best when they take charge of their own learning, but while young students are usually led by directed, compulsory education, adults must be self-motivated and rely on self-directed learning.

> > >

It is your mind, rather than circumstances themselves,
that determines the quality of your life. Your mind is the basis
of everything you experience and of every contribution
you make to the lives of others. Given this fact,
it makes sense to train it.
—Sam Harris

> > >

Have you accepted responsibility for your personal growth? Do you have a clear and practical plan for this area of your life? Your personal growth is not the responsibility of the HR department where you work. No one is going to force you to do it; devise your own plan.

5. Learn to anticipate and reflect.

> "Experiences aren't truly yours until you think about them, analyze them, examine them, question them, reflect on them, and finally understand them." —Warren Bennis

Our lives will be greatly enhanced if we will learn how to *anticipate* and *reflect*. These two actions precede (anticipate) and follow (reflect) experiences; they position the learner to reap the maximum benefit from experience.

Anticipate—*Before* you experience something, think about what you are about to do. Why are you doing it? What do you hope to accomplish? Anticipation helps us understand the context for action so we can maximize experiences.

Reflect—*After* you experience something, contemplate what happened. What did you learn? What should be the follow-up? Reflection helps us to make sense of experiences.

The 10/60/30 concept

This notion suggests that in all of life's experiences you should allocate or devote a certain percentage of your time to three elements: anticipating (perhaps 10%), the actual experience (perhaps 60%), and reflection (perhaps 30%). The percentages can be adjusted for different activities.

For instance:

When reading a book—spend a few minutes anticipating what you hope to learn from the book, read the book, and then reflect on what you have learned. This ration might be 5/60/35.

Prior to a business appointment—think about what you hope to accomplish in the meeting, have the meeting, and then reflect on what transpired and the next steps of action. These percentages might be 15/65/20.

Prior to a vacation—research where you're going, bon voyage, and at the end of each day codify your thoughts about your experiences. These percentages might be 10/70/20.

Several years ago I was in New York City and planned to spend an afternoon at the Museum of Natural History. When I arrived at the museum I sat in the rotunda and spent about 15 minutes planning my visit (anticipate). I decided to spend most of my time in a special exhibit that featured the life and work of Margaret Mead, one of our nation's finest anthropologists. Then, I spent about an hour enjoying the exhibit. Before leaving the museum, I returned to the rotunda and for 20 minutes I reflected on what I had just learned and recorded my thoughts in my journal.

One thought I recorded that day changed my concept of teamwork. Mead said, "Never doubt, that a small group of committed, thoughtful citizens can change the world. Indeed, it's the only thing that ever has."

>>>

Follow effective action with quiet reflection.
From the quiet reflection will come even more effective action.
—Peter Drucker

>>>

Your learning will be greatly enhanced if you devote even a small amount of time to both anticipation and reflection.

6. Record your thoughts.

Maintain a journal where you write down significant thoughts. This is not a *diary* where you record your history, and it's not a *personal organizer* where you keep your to-do list. It's a *thought journal* where you record what you're learning and what is "becoming more clear" to you.

For instance, when you finish reading a book, record what you learned. When you hear an interesting phrase or anecdote, write it down. Maintain a list of vocabulary words you're working on. Have a designated place in your journal to update your thought pipeline.

The physical act of writing is important. It's been said that writing something down is the equivalent to hearing it six times. Stephen Covey says, "Writing bridges the conscious and subconscious mind. Writing is a psycho-neuromuscular activity that literally imprints the brain."

Writing helps us codify our thoughts; putting thoughts on paper forces us to express what we have learned and increases retention. A.K. Chesterson said, "Thoughts disentangle themselves over the lips and through the fingertips."

Maintaining an active thought journal has changed my life. I am a better person today because I started journaling in 1990. If I had started when I was in high school (the late 1960s), I would be a much better man than I am today. I cannot stress this enough—if you incorporate this one practice into your life, the process will change your life.

In his must-read book, *Where Good Ideas Come From*, Steven Johnson talks about the Enlightenment-era practice of maintaining a "commonplace" book.

> "The great minds of the period—Milton, Bacon, Locke— were zealous believers in the memory-enhancing powers of the commonplace book. In its most customary form . . . it involved transcribing interesting or inspirational passages

from one's reading, assembling a personalized encyclopedia of quotations."

7. View yourself as unfinished.

"We all differ in what we know, but in infinite ignorance, we are all equal." —Sir Karl Popper

Few things will stunt learning more than intellectual arrogance accompanied by a false sense of knowing-it-all. Sadly, some people live as if they have maxed-out their learning—there's little more to learn, do, or become.

Instead, we must view ourselves as unfinished—a work in progress; we all live in what Popper calls the realm of "infinite ignorance." A healthy, proper approach to learning is predicated upon a deep humility based on the fact that we know and understand so little.

Consider the following two graphics. In each one, the outer circle represents all that a person can learn and become. The inner circles represent

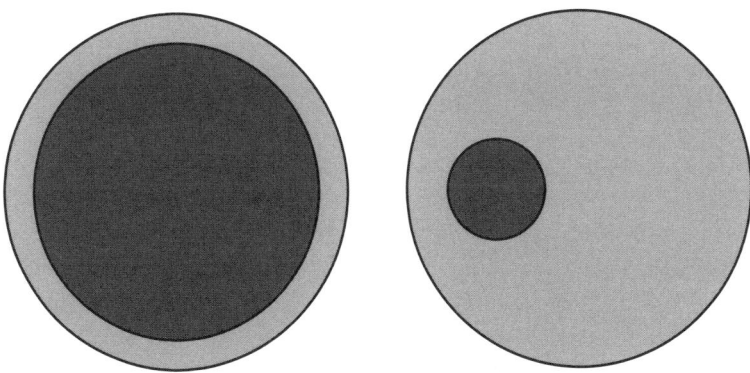

two different attitudes toward this vast unknown. The person represented by the graphic on the left thinks, "I have become just about all that I can become; I have learned just about all that I need to know." The person represented by the graphic on the right thinks, "There's so much to learn and I have so much potential that remains untapped—if I lived to be 200 years old I could only scratch the surface."

All innovation, creativity, and learning lie in the realm of the unknown.

>>>
Potential principle: We are all embryonic;
we can grow and develop and release more potential
and develop more talents.
—Stephen Covey

>>>

John Gardner challenges us with this thought: "Most men and women go through their lives using no more than a fraction—usually a rather small fraction—of the potentialities within them."

Heil, Parker, and Tate encourage us to always examine our thinking: "Continuously testing the quality of our thinking must become a fundamental part of every improvement process. Good questions to ask include:

·   In the last six months, what have I changed my mind about?

·   What have I learned this month that makes my actions last month less effective?

·   What about my present mindset do I find myself questioning recently?

·   Who thinks very differently than I do? What have I learned from them lately?"[6]

8. Don't overestimate your abilities.

"Often, we form our impressions not globally, by placing ourselves in the broadest possible context, but locally, by

comparing ourselves to people who are 'in our same boat.'"
—Stouffer

Lake Wobegon is a fictional town in Minnesota, said to have been the boyhood home of Garrison Keillor, who reports the news from Lake Wobegon on the radio show "A Prairie Home Companion."

The series introduced what has been called "the Lake Wobegon Effect" which Wikipedia defines as, "A real and pervasive human tendency to overestimate one's capabilities and achievements relative to others." It is named after the fictional town where "all the women are strong, all the men are good looking, and all the children are above average."

For instance, the residents of the town are convinced that the valedictorian of their high school must be the smartest student in the nation. But when the student goes to the state university, it becomes obvious that there are many "smartest students in the nation," and in fact, the Lake Wobegon student is quite average.

When we overestimate our abilities and achievements relative to others, we succumb to the Lake Wobegon Effect.

A subtle variation occurs when someone does excel in one particular area of life—but only one area of life—but thinks that his expertise in that one area makes him superior to others. For instance, you may be a good lawyer, perhaps one of the best in your town. But have you worked with attorneys in New York and London? Have you conversed with law professors from Ivy League schools? And, though you may, indeed, excel in law, is that your only area of expertise? Have you spent time with a gifted poet, a world-class scientist, or a Master of Wine?

The solution to this limited and myopic view of life, as Stouffer suggests, is to "place yourself in the broadest possible context." This will provide a more realistic setting in which to evaluate yourself, and it may motivate you to strive for higher goals.

9. Develop your personal intellectual nutrient base.

On a regular basis, you need to feast on proven sources that provide "food for thought." You need to define and utilize a personal intellectual nutrient base that provides a steady source of significant thoughts.

My intellectual nutrient base includes:

- *The Economist*—a weekly magazine published in England. It is inaccurately named because it covers much more than economic issues; it addresses issues in politics, world affairs, the arts, science, and other areas.

- *The New York Times*—one of the greatest newspapers in the world. It has a huge staff of top-of-class journalists that write about global issues. I read the weekend edition.

- *The Smithsonian* and *National Geographic*—monthly periodicals.

- I read one non-fiction book a week.

- TED talks, lectures, and debates available on You Tube.

10. Discover and fine-tune your personal learning style.

> "You must know yourself to grow yourself. Knowing yourself
> is like reading 'you are here' on a map."—John Maxwell

How do you best learn? When and where do you learn best? Each of us has a uniquely optimum learning style. It may take several years for you to experiment with different options and find what works best for you.

Here's what works best for me.

Relative to my optimum learning environment

- I learn best in a quiet environment. I do not read, think, or memorize well in a noisy setting.

- My most productive learning space is my home study.

- In my home study I have three learning stations—my desk, a couch, and a chair. Just moving from one station to another helps me stay fresh. I'll work in one area until my attention begins to wane and then move to another station.

- I don't have an optimal time of day in which I learn best; I can engage at any time.

Relative to reading

- Instead of reading one book at a time, I always have three books that I'm reading. I'll read one for 30 minutes then switch to another and then another. The three books are usually vastly different in topic and writing style.

- I don't read large books on a single topic. Someone recently gave me a copy of *Steve Jobs* by Walter Isaacson. While I appreciate the gift, I will not read the book because I don't want to read 575 pages on one person. I'm interested in Steve Job's life, but I'm not *that* interested.

- If I read 60 minutes a day, I can read about three books a month. My goal is to read 52 books a year, so I read more on vacations and holidays.

- I have developed a method for processing the books I read. (See chapter four.)

Relative to travel

· My wife and I try to visit one new country every year.

· I apply the 10/60/30 rule to our travels.

Relative to general learning

· I am visual learner; I learn best by seeing instead of just hearing.

· I am a generalist, not a specialist, so I would rather learn a little about a lot of things than a lot about a few things.

What are some unique characteristics of your personal learning style?

11. Consider the lens through which you see the world.

> "We must look at the lens through which we see the world, as well as at the world we see, because the lens itself shapes how we interpret the world." —Stephen Covey

For better and for worse, we all have what psychologists call "personal constructs"—frames of mind through which we see ourselves and others. I'll adopt Covey's metaphor and call them lenses. Our lenses act as both frames and cages: they add focus and definition to our view of the world, but they are often so rigid that they restrict our view and perspective. They come with a set of presuppositions and assumptions that anesthetize the mind.

Psychologist Brian Little says, "If you have a construct system that is primarily centered around one core construct, this means that you have very little wiggle room when that construct is challenged. You have limited degrees of freedom in navigating your world."

For instance, someone may view life through a single "intelligent or stupid" lens—that is, every person and all human actions are lumped into one of these two categories. Another primary lens divides everyone by "Republican or Democrat" in which everyone falls into one of those two groups and *only* those two groups, and with preconceived opinions about both.

I was raised in a strict, somewhat legalistic Christian family. We had one core construct: everyone was either a Christian or a non-Christian; you were either one of us or one of them, and all unbelievers were suspect. When I started college at the University of Texas at Austin, I tried to discern which category each professor was in. I was skeptical towards those who were "one of them" and those I was uncertain about. How foolish. When studying mathematics, or German, or 16th-century counterpoint, what difference does the teacher's religious beliefs make?

Early in life, our lenses were crafted by our family of origin and our local environment. In essence, we inherited our first set of glasses.

Have you ever analyzed and critiqued the lenses through which you see the world? It is a healthy thing to do. Doing so may

- cause you to change

- solidify your perspective

- help you understand others

- encourage you to embrace diversity

- be an antidote for intellectual apathy

This type of analysis is not for the faint of heart, but it's necessary if you want to free your mind from the constraints of constructs.

>>>

Before I finish this chapter I want to introduce two simple tools that I use to help codify what I'm learning: a personalized dictionary and a personalized dates-to-remember chart.

Personalized dictionary

When I hear or read a phrase or word I'm unfamiliar with I enter it into my personalized dictionary. Obviously, this list does not include all the words I know, it only lists new words that I'm learning. You can set up a file in Microsoft Excel or Apple Numbers that will automatically alphabetize your entries. I also have a column to record how I first used the word in a conversation.

Dates-to-remember chart

When I read or hear of a historic event, I add it to my personalized chronology chart. I also record how this date became of interest; perhaps I read a book about it or heard of it in my travels. I also keep this chronology in an Apple Numbers file. It will automatically arrange the dates in ascending order, though I have to keep two files, one for A.D. dates and one for B.C. dates.

When we consistently engage in lifelong learning we will become slightly different and slightly better over time.

LIFELONG LEARNING IS MORE DOABLE THAN YOU THINK—10 ACTIONS THAT WILL ENHANCE YOUR LEARNING

Fortunately, lifelong learning is readily accessible and absolutely attainable. It's not like you're going to have to take on a second job or change careers. It will easily fit into your current life and routine. It's doable. Just develop a few new habits and you'll quickly start reaping positive results.

In the last chapter we discussed 11 prerequisites to lifelong learning. Now let's consider how to do it. Here are 10 clear strategies that will enhance your learning.

1. Pursue a broad education.

When Peter Drucker was asked to name one thing that would make a person better in business, he responded, "Learn to play the violin." He was arguing for an expansive and extensive approach to education.

Many people limit their pursuit of knowledge to one narrow area or topic—usually their profession. While it's important to stay current professionally, it's best to take a broad approach to learning. If you're an architect, be good at what you do and stay current in your field, but also study art history, or gardening, or horology (the study of watchmaking), or other areas that are unrelated to your profession.

Studying many different topics will actually make you a better professional because it will make you a better, more well-rounded person.

Ferrazzi says, "Different experiences give rise to different tools. Take a deep and boundless curiosity about things outside your own profession and comfort zone."

2. Read.

> "One of the marvelous things about life is that any gaps in your education can be filled, whatever your age or situation, by reading, and thinking about what you read." —Warren Bennis

Are you in any of the following groups?

- 33% of U.S. high school graduates will never read a book after high school.

- 42% of college students will never read another book after they graduate.

- 80% of U.S. families did not buy a book last year.

- 70% of adults have not been in a bookstore or ordered a book online in the past 5 years.

[Source: Statisticbrain.com]

I hope you are not represented in these statistics.

The fact that you are reading this monograph indicates that you are literate. This is a good thing, but not sufficient. The critical question is not *can* you read but *do* you read? Mark Twain observed, "Those who do not read have no advantage over those who cannot read." I would add: but those who do read are better off than those who can read, but do not.

When was the last time you read an intriguing book that fed your mind and added value to your life?

>>>

Reading is your first line of defense against an empty head.
I read for a lot of reasons, pleasure being the least of them.
—Twyla Tharp

>>>

The potential benefit of reading regularly is astonishing. If you read 60 minutes a day, you could read one book a week, four books a month, 52 books a year, and 520 books in 10 years. That would change your life. If you read 520 books, in a world in which the average person reads less than a book a year, you would develop a decisive advantage in life.

Read widely and think deeply. Read as if your life depends upon it.

3. Memorize.

Knowledge without memory is useless. It doesn't matter how many books you have read, documentaries you have watched, or lectures you have heard—if you cannot remember what you have learned, there is little long-term value.

>>>

How we perceive the world and how we act in it are products
of how and what we remember. Memory training is about
nurturing something profoundly and essentially human.
—Joshua Foer

>>>

Learning without memorizing is like having a computer without a hard drive. Every time you shut it off, all your work is lost. When you turn it back on, you have to start all over. In like manner, if acquired knowledge is not reinforced and memorized at some level (conceptually or literally), then you'll have to relearn the information.

Granted, some data is best stored and then retrieved only when needed—there's no need to memorize all the telephone numbers in your personal data base—but there is tremendous value in memorizing key concepts and thoughts. It keeps us mentally sharp, we can more easily meditate on thoughts we have memorized, and we'll have a ready supply of concepts and wisdom that we can apply in real-life situations.

You'll need to craft a personalized memorization system that works for you.

- How are you going to organize the material? Some people use note cards. I use software called Evernote so I can access the information on all my digital devices.

- When will you focus on memorizing? It takes me 25 minutes to drive to work, so that becomes an ideal time to memorize.

- How often do you codify new material to memorize? I try to create a new file each week.

Find out what works for you, and then develop an ever-expanding collection of thoughts and ideas that you memorize.

4. Travel extensively.

Henry Thoreau said, "One sees the world more clearly if one looks at it from an angle." When we travel, we see things "from an angle," and the further we travel from home, the more severe the angle.

For instance, if you live in Dallas, Texas, and you travel to Houston, Texas, you'll see things differently, but not by much. Visit New York City, and you'll experience a significant change in culture. Cross the Atlantic Ocean to Paris, and you'll be even more challenged. Travel to India, and you may think you're on a different planet.

And there's a difference between being a tourist and a traveler. Tourists are satisfied to see the sights; a traveler wants to experience the culture. A tourist takes an air-conditioned bus from one site to the next and returns to the hotel to indulge in familiar accommodations. A traveler takes the local bus and stays in the same hotel that the natives do.

> > >

Travel is fatal to prejudice, bigotry, and narrow-mindedness.
Broad, wholesome, charitable views of men and things
cannot be acquired by vegetating in one little corner
of the earth all one's lifetime.
—Mark Twain

> > >

As of 2015, Mary and I have traveled to 43 countries, most of them multiple times. I remember enjoying a picnic lunch of cheese, bread, and wine on a Swiss hillside while watching a farmer cut grass with a sickle. When visiting the Hermitage Museum in St. Petersburg, Russia, we gained access to a room full of famous paintings that are usually off-limits to the public because they are disputed assets related to unresolved war reparations from World War II. We had lunch in a cafe in Marrakesh, Morocco, that was blown up by terrorist the following month. I have seen the destitute in New Delhi and the well-to-do, out-of-touch in Paris. I was in a bus wreck on the road between Tbilisi and Kobuleti. A four-hour meal shared with friends in Palermo is a memory that still gives me pause.

According to travel guru Rick Steves, 80 percent of Americans do not hold a passport. That's sad.

Travel takes time and money, but it's worth the investment. You'll be stretched and challenged, and you'll learn more about the world in which you live. St. Augustine said, "The world is a book, and those who do not travel read only one page."

5. Pursue invigorating relationships.

Be intentional about spending time with engaging, fully-alive individuals, and be deliberate in your conversations with them.

You will benefit from both distant mentors (people you respect but do not know personally) and personal mentors (people you respect and interact with on a consistent and intentional basis). One of my distant mentors is Peter Drucker. I never met him and he is now deceased, but I have learned much from his life, primarily through his writings. I also have personal mentors—men and women with whom I interact on a regular basis.

Continually expand your network; don't spend all your time with the same people. Samuel Johnson set himself a rather lofty goal: "I look upon every day to be lost, in which I do not make a new acquaintance." We may not be able to meet one new person a day, but surely we can engage with at least one new person every week.

> > >

The work of the Roman biographer Plutarch is based on the premise that the tales of the excellent can lift the ambitious of the living. Thomas Aquinas argued that in order to lead a good life, it is necessary to focus more on our exemplars than on ourselves, imitating their actions as much as possible. The philosopher Alfred North Whitehead argued, 'Moral education is impossible without the habitual vision of greatness.'
—David Brooks, *The Road to Character*

> > >

When you meet with interesting people, have an agenda or else you may waste the opportunity by just talking about random, insignificant issues. For instance, you could ask: What is your favorite leadership principle? What are you currently working on? How do you stay emotionally and intellectually fresh? What advice can you give me about …?

6. Learn from successes and failures.

"Experience is not the best teacher; evaluated experience is." —John Maxwell

Learn from your successes

Do we learn more from studying failures or successes? Obviously, we learn from both, but often we analyze our failures and merely celebrate our successes. But the most valuable lessons may come from studying our successes. Here's why.

You cannot infer success by studying failure and then inverting it. Of all the different ways to perform a certain task, most of them are wrong. Failure reveals what does not work, but it will not tell what does work. That's why you cannot learn much by studying failure.

You need to carefully analyze successes because it is often difficult to determine exactly why something was successful; cause and effect are hard to establish. For instance, was the workshop you sponsored well attended because of the topic, the speakers, or because it was held in the Caribbean? When you do succeed, create hypotheses about why it may have happened and test them to confirm accurate correlations.

Also, carefully reflect on your early successes because they may mislead you. Po Bronson says, "Failure is hard but success can be far more dangerous. If you're successful in the wrong thing, the mix of praise and money and opportunity can lock you in forever."

Learn from your failures

View failures and mistakes as both unavoidable and acceptable. Management consultants Pfeffer and Sutton say, "Setbacks and mistakes should be viewed as an inevitable, even desirable, part of being action oriented. The only true failure is to stop trying new things and to stop learning from the last effort to turn knowledge into action."

If we are afraid of failure, we will never move beyond our safe zone; we will never leave sight of the shoreline for the vast ocean. Instead of thinking, "Failure is not an option," think "Failure is an option, and there's a good probability that it will happen."

When you fail, look for causes, not excuses. Analyze what happened, identify some causes, learn, and adjust.

Although failure is a natural byproduct of living an aggressive life, never be cavalier about failure and don't romanticize it. Failure is not acceptable if it is the result of slothfulness, poor planning, or poor execution.

Are you failing enough?

In 1952, Drs. Watson and Crick discovered DNA. Dr. Watson calmly proclaimed, "I have discovered the source of life." Their findings were published in an 874-word paper. Years later, Dr. Crick acknowledged that some of his postulations were off-beat and speculative. "But," he told the *Associated Press* in 1994, "a man who is right every time is not likely to do very much."

Picasso used up no less than eight notebooks just for preliminary sketches of his revolutionary painting, "Les Demoiselles d'Avignon," before he was satisfied.

Thomas Edison, when commenting on his experiments to invent the light bulb said, "I have not failed, I've just found 10,000 ways that won't work."

Winston Churchill said "Success is the ability to go from failure to failure without losing your enthusiasm."

Avoid the hot-stove effect

The hot-stove effect was first proffered by humorist Mark Twain:

"We should be careful to get out of an experience only the wisdom that is in it and stop there lest we be like the cat that sits down on a hot stove lid. She will never sit down on a hot stove lid again and that is well but also she will never sit down on a cold one anymore."

Throughout life, we should be careful to not overreact to painful experiences. Failures, embarrassing moments, and hurtful events, if not properly processed, can have an inordinate impact on our lives and dissuade us from "jumping on the stove" again.

Carefully study and analyze all of your experiences and put them in proper perspective. Experiential learners are particularly susceptible to the hot-stove effect; it can cause them to be inordinately risk-averse.

For example:

- You may abandon a helpful technology because your first experience with it was distasteful.

- Some divorcees resist the thought of marrying again because of the hurt they sustained in a former marriage.

- Not being accepted into your school of choice may discourage you from pursuing formal education.

I have been a public speaker and teacher for 30 years, but an embarrassing moment in high school might have derailed this aspect of my career.

In high school, I was the vice president of my senior class. Once, when speaking before the student body, I planned on using the phrase "hook, line, and sinker," as in, "He was so naive that he swallowed it hook, line, and sinker." But in my speech the phrase came out "sink, line, and hooker."

My classmates were unmerciful. Unfortunately, no one helped me process what had happened. Fortunately, I thought carefully about the incident by myself and decided that though it was a bad experience, it need not be a life-changing one. I avoided the hot-stove effect.

7. Solicit a personal coach.

Studies show that if you want to get in good physical shape, working with a personal trainer is more beneficial than working out alone or even with friends. Personal accountability to a trained expert who provides informed feedback is invaluable.

Likewise, having a life-coach is perhaps the quickest and best path to self-awareness and personal development.

It's helpful to know the difference between a mentor and a coach.

A mentor says, "I do; you watch and learn."

A coach says, "You do; I will watch and give immediate feedback."

For instance, consider a baseball player who wants to improve his batting skills. He considers Babe Ruth his mentor, so he watches tapes of Babe swinging at the ball and tries to emulate his motions. Babe swings, the aspiring player watches and learns.

But a batting coach will hand the player a bat, observe him in action, and then give immediate feedback.

>>>

Living life without ever getting feedback is like bowling through a curtain that hangs down to knee level.

>>>

Can you sense how much more effective coaching is? It's amazing how much improvement can come from just a few sessions with a competent coach.

You may want to hire a professional coach or solicit the input of a wise and trusted friend or colleague. Identify someone you respect and trust and ask, "I hold you in high regard. Would you please help me by evaluating my life and then give me frank and honest feedback?"

Coaching can help us hone both professional and life skills.

I once made these observations to two different friends who had solicited my input on their life skills.

> "You lack personal discipline. It affects every area of your life. You're deep in debt, you sleep too much, and you're usually late for appointments. Until you remedy this core problem, you'll never become all that you can be."

It took several years, but she changed and became a much better person.

> "You have two main areas to work on, both regarding personal communication: you don't filter your speech and you don't listen well. Before words come out of your mouth, think about what you're about to say: Does this make sense? Is this the right time to speak? Analyze every thought before it becomes speech and vigorously edit. And, become a good listener."

He took my advice and became a much better person.

What I'm describing is customized learning. It is very effective because we are often oblivious to our personal weaknesses. Even if we are aware of areas that need to change, the other ways of learning that I've suggested in this chapter (reading, traveling, memorizing, and being with invigorating people) may not specifically address the issues.

8. Learn from others and from your own experiences.

Knowledge can come from many sources. Secondhand knowledge is what we learn from others; experiential knowledge is what we learn by observing, analyzing, and making sense of our own life experiences. Pursue both.

Secondhand knowledge allows us to benefit from what others have learned. What might have taken someone years to learn (and often through formidable adversity), we can learn quickly and painlessly. For instance, Dan and Chip Heath, two brilliant professors, wrote a book on effective communication titled *Made to Stick*. I paid $14 for the book and read it in six hours—a small price to pay for what took them years to learn and codify.

Firsthand knowledge comes from our own experiences, but I'm often surprised to discover how little people learn from their own experiences.

I once met with a young friend who had recently been fired from his job. After listening to his story and empathizing with him, I asked, "What have you learned from this difficult season of your life?" He had no answer. He had not even thought about what he could learn from what happened. What a waste.

9. Maintain a bucket list.

A bucket list is a list of things you want to accomplish in your lifetime. They are typically out-of-the-ordinary experiences—not mundane, ordinary, predictable ones. For instance, you wouldn't include "maintain personal health" on your bucket list or "buy a car"; but you might include "tour Europe" or "plant a vineyard." And, they are usually big, challenging goals (get my pilot's license) and not small, simple activities (buy a water bed).

Most people think a bucket list is just for old people: "I'm 70 years old. What do I want to do before I die? On my deathbed, what will I regret having not done?" But a broader perspective would suggest that everyone should have a bucket list and that the earlier you start your list, the better. For instance, consider the exploits of John Goddard.

An article in the March 24, 1972 issue of *Life* magazine featured John Goddard who, at age fifteen, wrote down 127 goals he wanted to accomplish in his lifetime.

Included in his goals were: climb Mounts Kilimanjaro, Ararat, Fuji, McKinley (and thirteen others); visit every country in the world; learn to fly an airplane; retrace the travels of Marco Polo and Alexander the Great; visit the North and South Poles, Great Wall of China, Taj Mahal (and other exotic areas); become an Eagle Scout; dive in a submarine; play flute and violin; publish an article in *National Geographic*; learn French, Spanish, and Arabic; milk a poisonous snake; read the entire Encyclopedia Britannica; and other goals, similar in variety and scope.

At age 47, Goddard had accomplished 103 of these goals and was in the process of completing several others. Goddard was neither wealthy nor gifted when he began his amazing saga of adventure and accomplishment. He was just a young boy who believed all things were possible and that he could set and accomplish goals.

I wonder how many of those experiences he would have had if he had not formally expressed them as goals.

Goal-setting is good; it clarifies intent and focuses resources.

What happens if you don't set and pursue concrete goals? You will likely drift through life, accomplishing little; you'll not reach your potential, you'll underutilize your gifts and squander your resources. In other words, if you aim at nothing, you will hit it.

Maintaining a bucket list and working hard to accomplish every item will enhance your pursuit of lifelong learning. It will expose you to new ideas and experiences. Consider what Goddard must have learned "along the way" as he pursued his extraordinary goals.

10. Learn from significant thoughts.

Significant thoughts can change your life.

Call them what you will—wise sayings, proverbs, maxims, aphorisms, adages, quotes—they are concisely written or spoken linguistic expressions that are especially memorable because of their meaning or structure. They are distilled wisdom—important thoughts reduced to a few choice words.

How are famous sayings formed? Who vets all the statements uttered by mankind and decides which ones become timeless and often transcendent? Interestingly, there's no selection committee and no official vote is taken. A combination of time and human censorship has filtered and culled mankind's thoughts, and what has survived are nuggets of truth.

Here are some suggestions on how to benefit from significant thoughts.

1. Constantly search for significant thoughts.

In your reading and conversations, be on the lookout for thoughts that matter. Just this week, while reading a book, I discovered this Chinese proverb: That the birds of worry and care fly above your head, this you cannot change; but that they build nests in your hair, this you can prevent.

2. Write them down.

If you don't write the thoughts down, you'll lose them. If necessary, write them on a scrap piece of paper until you can transfer them to your thought journal. There's even value in the physical act of writing.

3. Memorize them.

This is the most important step, but is often neglected. When you memorize a statement, it finds a place in your mind and becomes available for reflection and application. Knowledge without memory is useless.

4. Share them.

Significant thoughts make for interesting conversation. The next time you're with friends, introduce a noteworthy thought into the conversation and let everyone talk about it. Getting other people's input will deepen your understanding and appreciation of the thought, and they will benefit from the conversation. Recently, at a family dinner, I proffered this thought and we had an interesting and vigorous conversation about it, "I want to live so that my life cannot be ruined by a single phone call."—Federico Fellini

5. Apply them.

One of the great moments of life is when we experience propositional truth—when a significant thought impacts us in a practical way. Through the years, my life has been molded and changed for the better as I have allowed important thoughts to do their work on my mind. My worldview has been enhanced, I am more competent, and more fully alive because I have studied important thoughts.

I even started a blog site—*Think With Me*—where I post musings on significant thoughts and invite my readers to interact with them. It is located at www.donmcminn.com.

> > >

To live in the presence of great truths and eternal laws,
to be led by permanent ideals, that is what keeps a man
patient when the world ignores him and calm and
unspoiled when the world praises him.
—Epictetus

> > >

Here are 15 wise sayings that have changed my life.

1. All of us are smarter than any one of us. —Unknown

This thought changed my leadership style from authoritarian to collaborative. If I surround myself with smart, engaged people, I want to hear what they think. Any idea or plan, when submitted to the wisdom of others, will be improved.

2. Seek first to understand, then to be understood. —Stephen Covey

This is the best thought on effective communication I have ever embraced. It made me a better listener and communicator.

3. Born originals, how comes it to be that we die copies? —Edward Young

Every human being is unique, but in the course of life we become homogenized. How sad. This thought started my journey into developing the concept of Signature Soulprint.

4. Without memory, knowledge is useless. —Daniel Taylor

Once I memorized this phrase, I understood the importance of memorization. If you don't remember important thoughts, they will have little impact on your life.

5. One of the marvelous things about life is that any gaps in your education can be filled, whatever your age or situation, by reading, and thinking about what you read. —Warren Bennis

This thought reignited my love for reading and solidified in my mind the value of reflection.

6. Most people worship the god of their fathers. —Unknown

What a thought-provoking statement.

7. Everyone is entitled to their own opinions but not to their own facts. —Daniel Moynihan

This statement clarified in my mind the difference between opinions and facts and the superiority of the latter. Emotions and opinions fluctuate but facts remain. I want to live my life based on facts.

8. One of the hardest things to do in life is to see ourselves as others see us. —Bill George

Self-awareness is a gift that few of us possess. I want to be self-aware.

9. The test of a first-rate intelligence is the ability to hold two opposed ideas in the mind at the same time and still retain the ability to function. —F. Scott Fitzgerald

When I first memorized this statement, I didn't fully understand it. But it has come to my rescue many times.

10. Five frogs sat on a lily pad. One frog decided to jump off. How many frogs are left? —Unknown

Unless they lead to action, good intentions can be feeble and misleading. I want to be an achiever; I want to get stuff done.

11. Some things are necessary but not sufficient. —Unknown

Erroneously, I am often satisfied with doing that which is necessary but I don't realize that more may be required.

12. The only things that happen naturally in an organization are friction, confusion and malperformance. Everything else is the result of leadership. —Peter Drucker

The health and growth of all organizations rises and falls on leadership. Period.

13. The best way to get a good idea is to have a lot of ideas. —Linus Pauling

A corollary thought is: "Coming up with new ideas is relatively easy. It's figuring out which of those ideas we should pursue that's tough." —Denny Post

But, first, start with a lot of ideas.

14. How many legs does a dog have if you call the tail a leg? Four. Calling a tail a leg doesn't make it a leg. —Abraham Lincoln

This quote is similar to a statement made by Philip K. Dick, "Reality is that which, when you stop believing in it, doesn't go away."

15. Your feelings are true but they are not truth.

We need to acknowledge feelings but at times be leery of them. Another great statement on emotions is, "Feelings are not an argument."

Fall in love with great ideas.

>>>

In this chapter I listed 10 ways to actively pursue lifelong learning. Develop a plan for personal growth that includes all areas. For instance:

1. I'm going to pursue the study of _____ because it is outside my current realm of interest and knowledge. (pursue a broad education)

2. I'm going to read these two books this month: _____ & _____. (read)

3. I'm going to adopt a system of memorization that works for me and begin immediately. (memorize)

4. In the next 12 months I'm going to take a trip to _____. (travel extensively)

5. I'm going to call _____ and meet with him or her in the next 10 days. I will be prepared to ask some key questions so I can learn from this person. (pursue invigorating relationships)

6. I'm going to analyze and learn from this recent personal success: _____. I'm going to analyze and learn from this recent personal failure: _____. (learn from successes and failures)

7. I'm going to solicit a personal coach to help me professionally and with life skills. (personal coach)

8. I will learn from others and from my own life experiences. In the next several days I will analyze and learn from this experience: _____. (learn from experiences)

9. I want to do the following 10 things before I die. (bucket list)

10. Here are several significant thoughts that I am going to meditate on: _____. (significant thoughts)

Five years from now, you are going to be the same as you are today, unless you invest in the 10 practical actions discussed in this chapter.

HOW TO GET MAXIMUM BENEFIT FROM READING

In the last chapter I wrote briefly about the value of reading. Here are some additional thoughts on how to learn from reading and a system I have developed that helps maximize the benefits I receive from reading.

1. Read.

Make reading a priority; otherwise you'll neglect it.

Make reading a regular part of your routine. Some people read daily, others read for longer periods of time on the weekend. My favorite time to read is when I first get home from work in the evening; it's a great way to relax and refocus.

Always have a book with you so you can take advantage of downtimes during the day; small increments of time add up quickly.

> > >
> What you are today and what you will be in five years largely
> depends on two things: the people you meet and the books you
> read. So it must be asked: What books are you reading?
> With whom are you developing a relationship?

> > >

2. Select good material that you can learn from.

There's a difference between reading for pleasure and reading to learn. I read the daily newspaper to relax and catch up on the news, but I don't read it to learn. I read a few novels every year, but I don't anticipate that I'm going to learn a lot; I read them for pleasure.

Determine that you are going to invest time in reading with the intent to learn.

It is often challenging to find good material that we can learn from. Don't underestimate how hard this can be; most printed material is intellectual cotton candy. Here are some suggestions for finding good material.

1. Get recommendations from friends who enjoy learning through reading.

2. Read book reviews (the Sunday edition of *The New York Times* has an entire section on book reviews).

3. Identify periodicals that feed your mind. I enjoy *National Geographic*, *Smithsonian*, and *Harvard Business Review*.

4. Identify authors who you enjoy reading. For instance, I buy everything Steven Johnson writes (recently, I read *How We Got to Now*).

Also, realize that information posted on the Web or social media probably does not have the same integrity as a book that has been well researched.

3. Discover your personal reading preferences.

You need to discover what style of books work for you. For instance, I don't enjoy reading a large book on a single subject; I don't have the interest or the patience. I'm a generalist so I would rather read three shorter books about three different topics than one long book about one.

Also, don't hesitate to stop reading a book if you lose interest in it. Normally,

I'll read at least the first 30 pages of a book, but if it hasn't grabbed me by then, I'll either put it aside or skim-read it.

4. Develop a process that will help you retain what you read—read and mark.

>>>

Your mental constitution is more affected by one book thoroughly mastered than by twenty books merely skimmed.
—Charles Spurgeon

>>>

I once asked a group of business executives, "Who has read Jim Collins' book, *Good to Great*?" About 70 percent of the group proudly raised their hands. I then asked, "Can anyone recall just one key principle from the book?" I got blank stares and silence filled the room. Finally, one man mumbled something about "that bus thing." Reading Collins' great book had no lasting value for these executives because they didn't retain anything.

I'll never forget that moment. It taught me that it's not sufficient to just read; we need a system that will help us solidify and retain what we learn.

I've developed the following system that works for me. Use it as a general template and craft your own system.

1. Before you start reading, take about 10 minutes to anticipate what you hope to learn. What is the topic? Why have you chosen this book or periodical? Who is the author? Why should you spend time reading this material? How might it impact your life? Study the table of contents to get an overview of the book.

2. Read the book with pen in hand. When you read something that speaks to you, circle or underline it and then make marks in the upper/outside corner of the page (one mark means "this is good"; two marks mean "this is

really good"; three marks mean "this is outstanding.") Also, in the margins, write key words or thoughts.

3. Each person has his own reading/attention span. Read until your mind begins to drift, and then set the book aside or switch to another book. I normally focus on three books at a time. I'll read one for 20 minutes, then switch to another for 20 minutes, etc. With practice, you can increase your ability to concentrate while reading.

4. Quickly find links between what you read and real life. How can the thoughts espoused in the book be lived out in real life? If often helps to share with others, what you have learned.

5. When you finish reading the book, put it aside for several weeks.

5. Journal key thoughts.

1. About three or four weeks after you have read a book, re-read it, focusing on those areas that you marked. This should take about 1/5 the amount of time it took you to read it the first time.

2. Record in your thought-journal significant thoughts and passages from the book. I can often tell how much I will learn from a particular book by noticing how many pages of my journal are filled with thoughts from the book. I recently journaled a rather insignificant book that I had read and it only took one page of my journal; I filled six pages with thoughts from Joshua Shenk's book, *Lincoln's Melancholy*.

3. My thought-journal is a nice leather-bound book with lined pages. Recent studies indicate that we learn more and remember more if we write long-hand rather than type information into a computer, so I still journal using paper and pen.

4. Set the journal aside for several weeks.

5. Re-read your journal entries and highlight salient thoughts, particularly those you want to memorize.

> >>
>
> I read transactionally: How can I use this? It's not enough for me to read a book. I have to "own" it. I scribble in the margins. I circle sentences I like and connect them with arrows to other useful sentences. I draw stars and exclamation points on every good page, to the point where the book is almost unreadable. By writing all over the pages, I transform the author's work into my book—and mine alone.
> —Twyla Tharp
>
> >>

6. Memorize key thoughts.

Knowledge without memory is useless, so you must commit to memorizing key thoughts and concepts. When committed to memory, thoughts will continue to grow, mature, and become clear through the years.

So, as you re-read your journal entries, highlight notable thoughts, particularly those that you want to memorize.

The key to memorization is repetition and review.

7. Apply knowledge to life.

You must bridge the knowing-doing gap because knowledge without application is minimally useful.

Authors Pfeffer and Sutton wrote a terrific book titled *The Knowing-Doing Gap: How Smart Companies Turn Knowledge Into Action* (2000). It's a great read that exposes a conundrum we all face: why do we have such difficulty in doing what we know we should do? Why do we know but we do not do?

8. Keep a record of the books you read.

It helps me to keep a written record of the books I have read, so every year I maintain a list of the books and a brief summary of each one. I rate each book based on how much I benefitted from reading it.

My goal is to read a book a week. Here's an example of my log from January to June, 2015.

Books read and processed in the first five months of 2015 The numbers in brackets represent how I rate each book on a scale from 1 (not good) to 10 (exceptional).

January

1. *Lying*—Sam Harris [8]. Don't ever lie. Honesty is a gift we can give to others.

2. *Waking Up*—Sam Harris [6]. Radical thoughts on spirituality and meditation.

3. *Personal* (fiction)—Lee Childs [4]. I don't learn much by reading fiction.

4. *Socrates*—Paul Johnson [6]. Socrates laid the foundation for absolute morality.

5. *The Economic Naturalist*—Robert Frank [6]. Most everyday enigmas involve an economic principle.

6. *Mastering the Rockefeller Habits*—Verne Harnish [6]. Good business principles revisited.

February

7. *Essentialism: The Disciplined Pursuit of Less*—Greg McKeown [6.5]. Good thoughts on focusing on essentials.

8. *I Am Pilgrim* (fiction)—Terry Hayes [6]. CIA-type thriller; though it is a long read (566 pages), it is a good read.

9. *Where Good Ideas Come From*—Steven Johnson [7.5]. Well-researched with lots of interesting stories. Just the chapter on The Slow Hunch makes the book worth reading.

10. *The Boys in the Boat*—Daniel James Brown [7]. Lessons learned from the rowing team that won gold at the 1936 Olympics.

March

11. *Me, Myself, and Us*—Brian Little [7]. An engaging psychology professor writes on important issues of well-being, personality, etc. Just the chapter on Personal Projects: The Happiness of Pursuit, is worth the cost of the book.

12. *The Millionaire Next Door*—Stanley and Danko [6]. Through extensive research, the authors analyze what the "typical" American millionaire family looks like. The results are surprising and encouraging.

13. *In The Kingdom of Ice*—Hampton Sides [8]. In 1879 the Jeanette set sail from San Francisco. Her crew hoped to be the first humans to reach the North Pole. This story is a testimony to the incredible perseverance embedded in the human psyche.

14. *How We Got to Now: Six Innovations That Made the Modern World*—Steven Johnson [9]. A totally fascinating and insightful book; a must read. A blend of science and history.

15. *Leadership and the Customer Revolution*—Heil, Parker, and Tate [8]. I read this book eight years ago and it still speaks to important leadership issues, particularly relating to how to delight customers.

April

16. *The Automatic Customer*—Warrillow [5]. A good book about a narrow

topic—how to make customers automatic.

17. *Get What's Yours*—Kotlikoff, Moeller, Solman [6]. The Social Security system is very complicated; this book helps answer major questions.

18. *Ethics (for the real world)*—Howard and Korver [8]. A thorough and practical book on ethics in both our personal and professional lives. A must-read book.

19. *The First 90 Days*—Watkins [7]. A must-read for everyone who is starting a new job or taking on a new role. "The actions you take during your first 90 days in a new role will largely determine whether you succeed or fail." (pg. 1)

20. *50 Rules Kids Won't Learn in School*—Sykes [4]. Written to teenagers but I can't imagine a kid reading this book. Sykes is very sarcastic and belittling in his approach. All I got were a few good quotes.

May

21. *The Road to Character*—Brooks [9]. A great treatise on character illustrated by a brief biography of major characters (Eisenhower, Augustine, Dorothy Day, and others).

22. *Stand Out: How to Find Your Breakthrough Idea and Build a Following Around It*—Dorie Clark [6]. I got a few new thoughts from this book.

Books that I skimmed

1. *Coming of Age in Samoa*—Mead [5]. Margaret Mead was one of our nation's greatest anthropologists, studying adolescent girls in Samoa. But, the book is tedious to read because of the large amount of detail given.

2. *How to Read and Why*—Bloom [5]. An erudite book on reading; a little beyond my understanding and interest.

Books that I bought, started to read, but did not finish because they are poorly written. (Some of these books were so bad that I threw them away; no use taking up limited shelf space.)

1. *Start With Why*—Simon Sinek [2]. Disjointed, confusing, just a combination of random thoughts.

2. *Kiss My Asterisk: A Feisty Guide to Punctuation and Grammar*—Jenny Baranick [2]. I couldn't get past the continued use of crude phrases and comments.

Conclusion

The following is from a Wikipedia article on lifelong learning. I think the article is spot-on and gives a good summary of what we've been discussing.

> "Lifelong learning is the 'ongoing, voluntary, and self-motivated' pursuit of knowledge for either personal or professional reasons. Therefore, it enhances social inclusion, active citizenship, personal development, and self-sustainability.

> "The term recognizes that learning is not confined to childhood or the classroom but takes place throughout life and in a range of situations.

> "During the last fifty years, constant scientific and technological innovation and change has had a profound effect on learning needs and styles. Learning can no longer be divided into a place and time to acquire knowledge (school) and a place and time to apply the knowledge acquired (the workplace). Instead, learning can be seen as something that takes place on an ongoing basis from our daily interactions with others and with the world around us. It can take the form of formal learning or informal learning, or self-directed learning."

Norman Maclean, author of *A River Runs Through It and Other Stories* and *Young Men and Fire*, lived to be eighty-seven years old. He lived life fully, as a woodsman, professor, and storyteller. The following excerpt was found in his files after his death, his exact intentions for it unclear. I think it summarizes the spirit and intent of this monograph and provides us with a nice way to conclude our discussion. His thoughts are well said and worth repeating.

"As I get considerably beyond the biblical allotment of three score years and ten, I feel with increasing intensity that I can express my gratitude for still being around on the oxygen-side of the earth's crust only by not standing pat on what I have hitherto known and loved. While the oxygen lasts, there are still new things to love, especially if compassion is a form of love."

I wish you well on your lifelong pursuit of learning.

End Notes

1) Maxwell, J. (2002). *The 21 Indispensable Qualities of a Leader*, Nashville: Thomas Nelson, pg. 144.

2) Bennis W. and Goldsmith J. (2003). *Learning to Lead*, New York: Basic Books, pg. xxi.

3) Clarke, B. and Crossland, R. (2002). *The Leader's Voice*, New York: Tom Peters Press, pg. 127.

4) Colvin, G. (2101). *Talent Is Overrated*, New York, Penguin Group, pgs. 9-10.

5) Kotter, John (1996). *Leading Change*, Boston: Harvard Business School Press, pg. 181.

6) Heil, G. and Parker, T. and Tate, R. (1995). *Leadership and the Customer Revolution*, New York: Van Nostrand Reinhold, pg. 59.

> > >

If you are interested in personal coaching in the area
of Lifelong Learning, contact Don McMinn at
don@donmcminn.com. Skype-based coaching sessions
are scheduled once a month and focus on
the disciplines outlined in this book.

> > >

Evergreen: Establish lifelong learning for life

We often know what we *should* do and even *how* to do it, but we simply don't follow through. Good intentions defeated by inactivity. The knowing-doing gap may be the biggest obstacle we face as we aspire to live a full and productive life. Sometimes, the gap between knowing and doing is more inhibiting than the gap between ignorance and knowing.

Knowing what to do is not enough; we must do. Establishing habits will help.

How long does it take to build a new habit?

Phillippa Lally is a health psychology researcher at University College London. In a 2009 study published in the *European Journal of Social Psychology*, Lally and her research team reported that it takes anywhere from 18 to 254 days for people to form a new habit.

Habits help, but they can be difficult to establish. A personal coach will help.

The value of having a private coach

The best and quickest way for an individual to negotiate long-lasting behavioral change is to hire a personal coach—someone who will guide your development and hold you accountable for mutually set goals.

Lifelong learning—make it a habit

This book listed 10 practical steps to cultivate lifelong learning:

pursue a broad education · read · memorize · travel extensively · pursue invigorating relationships · learn from successes and failures · solicit a personal coach · learn from others and from your own experiences · maintain a bucket list · learn from significant thoughts

The key is to make these 10 actions a regular part of your life—to make them *habits*.

Evergreen is a personal coaching program that specializes in lifelong learning. You'll talk once a month, via Skype, with an executive coach who will help you customize a personal training strategy based on the principles discussed in this book and help you accomplish it.

More information is available at donmcminn.com